A SNOWY DAY

Kate Petty

Illustrated by Jacqueline Wood

AWARD PUBLICATIONS

It's very cold tonight.
Robert has a hot drink
and a hot-water bottle.
Will it snow soon?

Robert looks out at the street.
It's snowing now!
He can see the first few flakes
in the light of the street lamp.

3

When Robert wakes up, his
room is full of light.
Everything is very quiet.
The snow must have settled.

Robert hardly recognises his
street now. It looks so white
and clean. Ginger is going
crazy in the snow!

Dad is not so pleased. His journey to work will be hard in the snow. Lots of trains and buses have been cancelled.

Robert helps Dad clear snow
off the car. Dad sprays
de-icer on the windscreen.
'Drive safely, Dad.'

Robert is wearing an extra
jersey and two pairs of socks.
Look at all the tracks in the
snow! Who has been here
before them?

Ouch! A snowball hits Robert
on the arm. Robert makes a
snowball to throw back. A
snowball fight has begun!
Mum keeps out of the way.

The children have cold hands
and feet. Some of them cry.
The teacher puts their gloves
on the radiator to dry.

Robert's class makes a
snowman and a snow-woman
in the playground. The snow is
quite wet and sticks together.

Each snowflake has six sides or points but no snowflake is the same as another.

Catch snowflakes on a dark glove or sleeve and look at them. You can see them more clearly with a magnifying glass.

Trace this hexagon on to white paper.

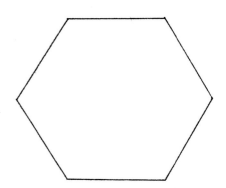

Use the hexagons to draw some of the snowflakes you have seen.

Now you can look at the patterns long after the snowflakes have melted.

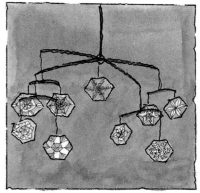

Mum has brought Robert's sledge to school. She pulls him to the park on it. His friends are going there, too.

Mum and Robert ride down the hill together. Robert can go down on his own. But it's hard work pulling the sledge uphill!

These mountains are covered with snow for much of the year. People come here to ski. Their skis glide over the snow.

Avalanche!
A huge weight of snow has broken away from the mountainside. The snow rushes downhill, flattening everything in its path.

A snowstorm is called a
blizzard. When the snow
comes down thick and fast
everything looks white.

Wind blows the snow into drifts. Sheep and lambs can be hard to find in snow-drifts. But their woolly coats often keep them warm under the snow.

polar bear

arctic fox

arctic hare

ptarmigan

stoat

The warm coats of these Arctic
animals help them to hide from
hunters in the snow.

These hunters build igloos
from ice when they are on
hunting trips.

Outside they need to wear furs
and skins. Inside they are
warm and cosy.

In the far North there is snow
on the ground for nine months
of the year. Some hot countries
never have snow.

Robert enjoys the snowy
weather while it lasts.

When the days get warmer,
there will be a thaw and the
snow will melt away.

snowy day words

avalanche

blizzard

igloo

skis

sledge

snowball

snow-drift

snowflake

snowman